25 Fires: A Call to What Comes Next

Eric S. Hoffman

This one is for my kids.

I. INFERNO

1.

We're better than this.

You know it.
I know it.
Your neighbors know it.
Your algorithms know it.

Our institutions are crumbling.
Schools are running on fumes.
Democracy sells to the highest bidder
And insulin costs more than your car.

We're better than this.

Every system we designed to serve society is
breaking down.
They've been corrupted.
Neglected.
Privatized.
Cannibalized.

And what are we left with?
Chatbots and call centers.
Data breaches and debt.

We're better than this.

We conjured a democracy from dust.
We came in from the wilderness
And built town halls, hospitals, and schools.

Not to make a few guys rich.

To teach us.
To treat us.
To feed us.
To lead us.

But now you call your congressman and they
just ask for a donation.
You call an ambulance and they ask you which
insurance plan you're on.

We're better than this.

We're on a 250-year experiment to prove a
simple premise:

"Everybody in here gets a shot."

But if we can't walk our own streets,
Or afford our own homes,
Then all the fancy words mean nothing.
And every broken system bleeds more life from
the American Dream.

We're better than this.

You know it.
I know it.
Everybody knows it in the quiet center of their
heart.

That's where truth still matters.
That's where faith still lives.
That's where courage waits to meet its moment.

And that's where the next revolution is going to
start.

2.

It's the economy, stupid.
Money isn't real anymore.

Your life savings is just a few keystrokes in a
database.
The government is forty trillion dollars in debt.

It's all a bit absurd.
But it's also deadly serious.

Because money is survival.
And not having enough means struggling in
ways parties and politicians don't seem to
understand.

Like listening to your kid cough because you
can't afford to take them to a doctor.
Or putting groceries back because your debit
card declined again.

So how are you supposed to get ahead these
days?
Trade crypto?
Sell drugs?

Most of us would gladly work an honest day for
an honest wage.
But honest wages don't buy houses anymore.
Honest wages won't pay for college for your
kids.
Honest wages don't return enough value to the
shareholders.
So the board's replacing your retirement
account with tips.

Welcome to the Class War.

Where banks won't call you back,
But billionaires can move the stock market with
a tweet.
Where three guys could end world hunger,
But they're more interested in measuring each
other's...

Rockets.

It's a late-stage Gilded Age that runs on gig
work.

But the tragedy is there's enough to go around.
More than enough.
We're the richest country in the world.
We could feed every child,
And fix every bridge,
And pay every schoolteacher a living wage.

But we don't.

And every day we don't is an admission that
we've lost our nation's soul.

But whether our future falls to the oligarchs,
Or rises with the citizens,
Is still an open question.

One that's up to We The People to decide.

3.

So where do you turn when institutions no
longer serve you?
What do you do when the economy has
squeezed you dry?

You blame your neighbor, of course.

His pronouns.
His politics.
His propaganda.
His pride.

He's everything that's wrong and nothing like
you.
He's the perfect outlet for all your anger,
Because he'll never change a goddamn thing.

He's a distraction.
A scapegoat while the wolves are at your door.

But don't take my word for it.
Ask your neighbor what he pays for childcare,
Or how much his rent went up this year.

I bet you'll find you've got many of the same
frustrations.
The same fantasies.
The same fears.

But waging culture wars is never going to solve
them.
Outrage is just a business now.
An algorithm
Inside an echo chamber
Run by a bot.

You could chase that dragon forever.

Or we can all grow the hell up.

The only way we'll ever solve our problems is by
facing them together.
We should all have freedom.
We all want justice.
Democracy is not a tool to keep each other
down.

And anyone that tries to tell you otherwise is lying.

Because they're afraid you'll see the power in the truth.

4.

Your mother is dying.

Her lungs are black with smoke.
Her blood runs thick with oil.
Her pores are clogged with batteries and plastic
bags.

Our civilization has pushed her to the brink.
Thirsty for energy.
Ravenous for growth.
We strip and extract and devour and burn.
It's the price of progress.
But what will be the lasting cost?

Maybe it's the parking lot that melts your child's
shoes.
Or the tap water that always tastes like
chemicals.
Maybe it's the snow that never came this winter.
Or the smog that never leaves.

There's a sense of doom that haunts us now.
An existential shame.

Some ignore it.
Some reject it.
It's too big.
Too costly.
Too late.

Meanwhile, Momma burns.
Like a house fire in slow motion.

But even while she suffers,
Mother Earth makes room for us to play.

To swim her ancient oceans.
To walk her sacred woods.
We climb on boulders.
We roll down hills.
We splash through puddles and feed the birds
because deep down,
We understand that this is home.

The only one we'll ever get.

So say a prayer for your dying mother.

Kiss her soil.
Caress her trees.
Accept that she's a challenge we're not ready for.
And hope one day we find the courage.

Or at least our children do.

5.

So how did it all come to this?

Failing institutions.
An economic house of cards.
How did hate become default and Earth become
an inconvenient truth?

It happened the way most things do.
Slowly.
Incrementally.
A million compromises piled up.

There were headlines.
There were warning signs.
But the alarm bells never quite got loud enough.
And everyone with power learned to look the
other way.

Our leaders have failed us.

Shamelessly, spectacularly so.

When we needed solutions,
They gave us scapegoats.
When we needed guidance,
They gave us greed.

They divided.
They exploited.
They hid behind the little flags on their lapels.
Now we drown in problems
While they campaign off the mess.

It's not working.

America is desperate for new leaders worth a
damn.
You know what they look like.
You may have seen some in your office, your
community, or your school.

They don't have all the answers.
They don't pretend to lead alone.
They're honest.
They're human.

They see the big picture and help the little guy along the way.

Because real leadership isn't about waging wars or cashing checks.
It's about standing up when everyone else lays down.
It's about sacrificing for people who can't pay you back.
It's about substance.
It's about heart.

It's about pointing at the elephant in the room and calling out:
"Let's eat this thing."

That's the kind of leader we need right now.
Hell, we need a million of them.

So grab a fork because we've got work to do.

II. SMOKE

6.

The phone rings and you flinch.

Is it your landlord?
The insurance company again?

You brace yourself and peek at the screen.
It's the school.
Shit.
Your kid must be sick.
Or in trouble.
Or God forbid-
Your mind drifts to dark places…

Welcome to the persistent trauma of our time.

We live in a state of hypervigilance.
Always bracing for the next catastrophe or
shock:

Mass shootings.

Overdraft alerts.
Hurricane warnings.
Presidential tweets.

They roll in around the clock
And keep our nervous systems in a state of
constant stress.
It's no wonder everyone's so anxious.
We live one BREAKING NEWS alert away from
World War Three.

So we cope.
However we can.
We make jokes about "adulting" and wonder
where our timeline went off track.
We swap horror stories at the pharmacy.
We call our therapist instead of eating lunch.

"This is fine."

Except it's totally not.
It's not healthy to flinch at phone calls and
doomscroll ourselves to sleep.
It's not normal to walk kids through lockdown
drills or fight with chatbots about your meds.

It's punishing.
It's demoralizing.
And it's every single day.

THIS IS NOT FINE.

This is a psychological reaction to a society
that's gone off the rails.

And the next time that damn phone rings,
I won't blame you if you scream until there's
nothing left.

7.

Is there anybody out there?
Is anyone actually home?

I wonder sometimes.
I scroll past all these comments and
conversations.
I swipe through photos and like updates about
your dog.

But it all feels... empty.

Like waving through a window when nobody's
waving back.

When was the last time you had a real-world
conversation with a friend?
How many family dinners dissolve behind the
blink of glowing screens?

We'll sit right next to each other on the couch
and scroll the night away.
It's no wonder we feel forgotten.
We've forgotten how to be present with each
other.

And this ache goes back.
Way back.
It's older than cities.
More fundamental than words.
It lives in the part of us that once sat shoulder-
to-shoulder around a fire.
That survived by hunting and cooking and
protecting each other as a tribe.

Now we work and date and learn and play
online.
We've engineered vast digital worlds to simulate
connection,
But they can't replace our need for eye contact
or human touch.

Those are the links that ground us.
The flash of recognition that says:
"I see you. I'm here too."

You can't Zoom it.
You can't swipe it.
You need to feel like you belong with people.
And losing that has wounded us in ways we
barely understand.

So if you're feeling lonely, you're not alone.

You're just a human.
Trying to remember what that word actually
used to mean.

8.

The easy thing to do is just check out.
I don't blame you.
Who has the stomach to get up each day and
give a damn?

Our leaders don't.
Our children can't.
Half the country just wants somebody to blame.

And so you check.
The fuck.
Out.

Don't @ me with this bullshit.
I've got three kids, two jobs, and a hernia I can't
afford to fix.
I just want to binge ice cream and Netflix all
night.
The problems will be there in the morning.
Hell, they'll still be there in twenty years.

When the world feels rigged and rotten,
Apathy becomes a strategy for self-defense.

You tried caring, but society didn't care back.
You tried fighting, but the bad guys always won.
So now you're finished.
Nothing left to give.

But let's be honest:
You're not apathetic because you don't care.
You're apathetic because you *do*.
Because it's become too punishing to get
invested.
It's easier to shrug things off and scroll on by.

Thoughts and prayers!

But apathy only works up until the chaos comes
to bite you.
Until the floodwaters are at your door.
Then you call for help,
And the only answer is that little voice inside.
Whispering a truth you've tried to bury all these
years:

It's up to you.

9.

Okay.

Let's come up for air.

If you're still here - thank you.
We just crawled through some heavy stuff
together.
Maybe I needed to say it.
Maybe you needed to hear it.
Maybe we can sit here for a minute and
meditate on something positive.
Something *good*.

Like hot coffee in the morning.
Cool pillows on a summer night.

Lacing up your favorite boots.
Cranking up your favorite song.
Cooking up some comfort food that always
tastes like home.

These are the simple joys that keep us smiling.
A million small reminders that:

We're better than this.

Even in our failures.
Even in our shame.

We're better than this because we have a choice
to be.
And every day we don't is a small betrayal of the
soul.

But tomorrow is another day.

Another chance to do what matters.
Another choice to do what's right.

I know it's hard.
I know it's thankless.
I know the headlines make you want to gouge
your eyeballs out with nails.

But tomorrow's gonna keep on coming.

And you can lay down and let it bury you,

Or you can stand up and take your swing.
Put your hips into it.
Punch right through the goddamn wall.

And then suddenly you're standing there,
Breathless,
Blinking in the sunlight, thinking:
Holy shit I did it.

And for once it was the world that flinched,
Instead of you.

10.

It's amazing what we all forget.

The human drama can be so noisy.
So relentless.
We lose sight of the big picture and where we
actually fit in.

Was this modern world inevitable?
Did everything just happen on its own?

Of course not.

It was forged by people.

Good people.
Bad people.
Selfish people.
Silly people.
People dreaming.
People scheming.

People following orders.
People breaking ranks.

Everything about this moment
Is covered in human fingerprints.
And now it's your turn.
What do you want to leave your mark on?
What do you think this world should be?

Bigger?
Braver?
Fairer?
Wiser?

All of these are possible.
Each is up to you.
But where to start?

Local.
Hopeful.
Simple.
Mindful.

Ask a question.
Solve a problem.
Push a boundary.

Plant a seed.

There are a million ways to make a difference at
your fingertips.
And each inspired action ripples outward with a
million more.

That's your power.

And when you finally step up and claim it,
You realize you don't have to try and change the
world.

You just have to try.

And the world will change.

III. EMBERS

11.

Bang.

The moment nothing became everything.
The birth of time and space and light.

You were there - in that cosmic soup.
A seed of possibility that needed fourteen
billion years to grow.

And grow it did.

Energy became matter.
Gravity became shape.
Reality raced outward,
Creating spacetime at the speed of light.

When you think about it, the universe is… too
much.

The scales are too big.

The stakes are too great.
There are more stars than all the grains of sand
on Earth.
But the nearest one would take a thousand
lifetimes just to reach.

What are you supposed to do with that?
How do you orient yourself beneath an endless
sky?

You trace your lineage through it.
The carbon in your bones.
The iron in your blood.
The atoms in your body forged inside exploding
stars.

You claim your role within it.
A clump of matter that grew conscious.
A universe that thinks and feels and wonders:
What it all might mean.

Maybe that's our place to stand.
Maybe that's the point.

But the next time you look up at the stars,

Consider it's a moment fourteen billion years in the making.

And you decide if that makes you feel big or small.

12.

You were born into a masterpiece.
Step back and soak it in.

Behold her crimson roses and her golden
autumn leaves.
Marvel at her tiger stripes and towering
bamboo.

Mother Nature doesn't just design, she dazzles.
She paints with butterflies.
She sings with birds.
She orchestrates a living symphony.
Ten million species, all in tune.

But behind the music lies a deeper message:

Adapt or die.
Evolve or go extinct.

For every flower and feather is the product of a
thousand generations.
Every wing and whisker tracks the progress of a
million lessons learned.

And the results?
Breathtaking.
Bees that break the laws of physics.
Spiders spinning silk as strong as steel.
Mother Nature's beauty is a living tribute.
Not to strength and cruelty,
But to creativity and fit.

So where do we fit in?
Evolution's greatest gamble?

Human beings were gifted with the tools to
build beyond her harsh selection.
But if we neglect to use them,
Mother Nature will destroy us all the same.

The blueprints are all around us.
In the courage of sea turtles.
In the patience of trees.
The species that survive are those that meet the
problems of the moment.

The ones that perish cling to stubborn habits
that no longer work.

Which are we going to be?
Dragonfly or dinosaur?
Sabertooth or swan?

The story of our future won't be based on how
we dominate the planet.

It will rest on how attentively we tune to
nature's song.

13.

The human story can be told in sticks and
stones.

Long before language.
Long before tools.
There was rhythm:
Some caveman pounding out a beat.

Maybe it started as a warning or a game.
Maybe he just liked to feel that echo bouncing
back.
Whatever the reason, that beat became our
calling.
A message to Mother Earth that we were
different.
We were more.

Then, we turned those sticks and stones against
each other.

Spears became swords became rifles became bombs.
We split the atom and set the sky on fire.

But as we mastered violence, something else emerged:

Rousing symphonies.
Timeless works of art.
Towering cathedrals.
More sticks.
More stones.

Human beings have always been creators.
We write and paint and sculpt and sing to express something we all feel,
But nobody knows how to say.

That we matter.

That this is not some cosmic joke.

And while our tools have evolved,
Our search for meaning has not.
Sticks and stones turned into cameras and keyboards.

The fire pit became the feed.

But it all serves the same impulse:
Our eagerness to matter.
Our quest to leave a mark.

We still fight.
We still bang drums.
We've done it forever and we probably always
will.

But we *are* different.

We *are* more.

We laugh.
We love.
We build.
We play.
We teach.
We reason.
We wonder.
We dream.

And somewhere in that rhythm,
Is the lesson that the universe set out to learn.

14.

And now we pray.

We close our eyes and seek that sacred place.
The place where silence speaks.
Where mystery meets truth.

We bring our hopes.
We bring our fears.
We bring our questions and regrets.
We pile them before an unseen altar,
Hoping to be met with grace.

It goes by many names.
It dwells in many houses, rituals, and books.
It is older than space.
Wider than time.
It is the voice that spoke existence into form.

Bang!

God the creator.
The answer to every question consciousness has
ever asked.

Where did we come from?
Why are we here?
What waits after all these fragile bodies fade
away?

God is where our understanding stops and faith
begins.
But no matter how we choose to seek it,
The source is something we will only ever find
within ourselves.

Because God is all of us.

God became us.

There's nothing else.
There never was.

God split singularity into multiples,
So we could explore contrast, creativity, and love.

And with this revelation,

All the ancient mysteries take on new light.

Like how to treat each other.
Why we're here.
What it means to be our own creators.
And how to walk a mindful path of duty,
possibility, and peace.

Some of us are not yet ready for this realization.
It takes courage to confront your own creation
in the mirror.

But if you're bright enough to see it,
If you're bold enough to claim it,
If you're brave enough to walk it.

Then your life becomes an act of worship.

More devout than any prayer.

15.

Now you'll have to sit with that a while.

Let the implications settle.
Give the transformation time.

Time.

The quiet river of experience.

Time turns seconds into centuries.
Time pounds mountains into dust.

Time is the lens through which everything we
do is focused.
Without time, there would be no galaxies.
There would be no memories.
There would be no beginnings, middles, or
ends.

And in that rhythm,

You discover that you only really have one
moment.

This moment.

Perched between the finite and forever.
A single opportunity to leave a mark on what
comes next.

You can long for the past.
You can dream of the future.
But you can only act now.

You don't get to try this moment later.
You don't get to save it for another day.

The moment arrives,
And then it is gone.
And what you do inside it is the force that
shapes your story.
Again and again and again and again.

Until you barely recognize what used to be.
Because you seized a million moments.

And created something new.

IV. KINDLING

16.

The ground feels steady again.
The jackhammer in your chest slows down.

You can sleep through the night.
Smile in the morning.
Back away from the ledge that no longer looms
to swallow you whole.

Imagine a world where daily survival isn't a
gauntlet.
Where stability is a place to start.

The HVAC hums.
The tap water runs clear.
The roof doesn't leak and kids eat breakfast
before school.

These are not luxuries.
These are the foundations.

The principles that guide our public policies
and goals.

You want safe streets?
Start with full bellies and warm beds.
You want economic growth?
Give people the bandwidth to plan beyond their
basic needs.

Because when everyone is drowning, they can't
do anything but fight for air.
But lift that insecurity away and something
magic happens:
Dignity comes back.
Humanity comes back.
Parents have time to raise their kids again.
Neighborhoods have space to breathe.

This is not radical.

It's not political.

It's doing the damn things people need to live
together.
And it's inevitable if we want to be a great
nation ever again.

It's time to put people first.
Not with lip service.
Not with trickle down charades.
With bricks and mortar.
With medicine and meals.

If we get the basics right, everything else gets
easier.

And we can dream big again,
Knowing that there's something there to catch
us if we fall.

17.

Now let's get to work.

Work that gives us purpose.
Work that makes us proud.

Strip away the bullshit and the buzzwords and
the brands.
Society runs on busting our ass:

Building.
Hauling.
Serving.
Fixing.
Cleaning.
Crafting.
Teaching.
Growing.

We don't do it for some ivory tower.
We don't do it for a stock price or IPO.

We do it for our families.
We do it for our communities.
We bring our skills and serve to make an impact
on the world.

But somewhere along the way,
Human capital became expendable.
Human beings became exploitable.
The working class got separated from the value
we create.

And in that disconnect, we lost our dignity.
But we can still take it back.
By fighting for each other.
And reclaiming what it means to work with
pride.

Like the bricklayer who owns stock in his own
skyline.
The teacher who owns a house next to the
school.
The nurse who gets to rest her feet.
The trucker who can see his kids.
The artist who shapes truth in ways an
algorithm never could.

That's what a human economy looks like.
The chance to make a living,
Without selling off your soul.

It applies to labor, and to leaders.
Yeah.
I'm talking to you too.

It's time to redefine success by putting people
over profits.
It's time to reinvest in those communities you
hollowed out.
It's time to put this system back in order.
And if you can't do that,
It's time to bring in someone else who can.

Because they're out there.

Building.
Hauling.
Serving.
Fixing.
Cleaning.
Crafting.
Teaching.

Working.

18.

I got you.

Right here.
Right now.
Right in the thick of this storm.

When you lose your way, I got you.
When you need a hand, I got you.
When you think you're alone, I fucking got you.

Because we're seamless, you and I.
Your battles are my battles.
My bread is your bread.
There are no strangers on this human journey.
We flow from the same ocean and wash up on
the same shore.

And when we get there,
We realize we were all just one big soul on
different paths.

It's a shame we couldn't see it sooner.
But what if we started to?
What if we did?

Imagine a world where kindness and
cooperation were instinctive.
Where everybody had each other's back.

We'd still need boundaries.
We'd still have challenges and fights.
But we could be mature about them.
We could frame our conflicts in a deeper truth
Of shared humanity and respect.

And in that future, everything is possible.

Every.
Single.
Thing.

It might take a generation.
It might take ten.
But we'll become unstoppable the day we finally
decide to work together.
And everything we've ever dreamed of will start
to feel like it's in reach.

Because I got you.
And you've got me.
And the whole damn world is in our corner.

Whether they understand it yet or not.

19.

Life finds a way.

She's relentless like that.

Through hailstones and hurricanes.
Wildfires and floods.
She adapts.
She evolves.
She experiments.
She endures.

And if we pay attention, we can learn to read her rhythms.
We can calibrate societies to align with nature's turn.

What might that look like?

Cities harmonized with seasons.
Infrastructure integrated with the land.

Rooftop gardens.
Boulevards that breathe.
The food is local.
The air is clean.

It's not a fantasy.

It's Philadelphia.
It's San Antonio.
It's Des Moines.

It's your own hometown:
Greener.
Cleaner.
Safer.
Stronger.

And as we harmonize, Mother Earth exhales.

Quietly.
Cautiously.
She opens up her canopy.
She stretches out her limbs.
New seedlings grow.
Old flocks return.

The line between nature and neighborhood
blurs.
And with it,
We reclaim our place in both worlds.

She'll always be a demanding mother.
She built this planet.
She's earned her wrath.

We can't escape the storms,
We can only choose the way we meet them.

Then pass these values to our children.

So they inherit harmony with home.

20.

Society is a body.
And democracy is a mirror.

It reflects everything about us.
The muscles we develop.
The wounds that we neglect.

Sometimes it's hard to look at.
Sometimes it makes us cringe.
But every leader rises out of that reflection:
Strongmen.
Conmen.
Revolutionaries.
Diplomats.

Right now, our leaders feel like chronic
inflammation.
They disrupt our systems.
They attack our flesh.
They represent a body that won't treat itself.

That's lived with pain so long we've all forgotten
how to heal.

But bodies can change.

Not by magic.
Not overnight.
By altering our habits.
By putting in the work.

Discipline and movement.
Sustenance and rest.
Stretching out old muscles.
Sharpening new skills.

It's up to We the People to reclaim the values of
a healthy nation.
And as our social body heals,
Democracy will reflect the change.

With competent candidates.
Dignified debates.
Evidence over ideology.
Public service over private wealth.

Only then
Will serious issues
Receive the serious treatment they require.

Give that a few cycles,
And we'll all have better healthcare.
Fairer taxes.
Stronger schools.

Crazy right?
But not impossible.
Not in a democracy.

Not when we treat our body like the temple it's
supposed to be.

V. SPARKS

21.

Take it back.

Your focus.
Your vision.
Your attention.

Take it back.

From the algos that entrap it.
From the egos that exploit it.
From the chaos that consumes it.
From the static and the noise.

Stop scrolling and start being present again.
The way we used to.
The way we're built to.
Remember you're a caretaker for something
sacred.
An ancient flame that sits behind your eyes.

Watching.

The patterns.
The machinery.
The flow.

Breathing.

In the body.
In the moment.
In the mind.

Recognizing.

The human nervous system underneath it all.
Eight billion kindred spirits.
Stumbling through it just like you.

When you reclaim your attention,
You activate the quiet piece of you that still
remembers.
You rise above the endless scroll and recognize:

We're better than this.

We're the torchbearers.

We're the universe.
We're a masterpiece.
We are God.

We're the ancient fires lit to contemplate our
own creation.

And it's up to us to see reality for what it really
is.

This.

22.

And now it's time to tell the fucking truth.

Not the slop that trends on Facebook.
Not the crap you think they want to hear.

The real shit.
Burning in your fingertips.
Bleeding from your chest.
The world is dying for some authenticity.
No one can even tell what's honest anymore.

So it's up to you.

To be a real one.

And understand that truth may be
uncomfortable.
Because truth confronts.
Truth exposes.
Truth is messy.

Truth is raw.

Truth asks hard questions and sees through the
easy answer.
Truth shakes old foundations.
Truth breaks new uncertain ground.

Truth feels lonely at first.
Everyone else is still pretending.
Still performing.
Still slapping filters over flaws.

But carry it long enough, and truth becomes
embodied.
You stop chasing validation.
You stop rehearsing every line.
Your shoulders drop.
Your vision clears.
You remember how to just…

Be.

And people notice.

Not all of them, but the ones who are ready.

They seize the chance to put their own mask
down.
To speak plainly.
To stand tall.

And before long, the lies all start to sound
ridiculous.
The talking heads run out of air to breathe.
The paper kings collapse beneath their own
illusion.

Because their world is built on nothing.

And truth will outlast every one.

23.

You always have a choice.
You have a million choices.

You can choose to chase temptation.
You can choose to do what's right.
You can choose happiness.
You can choose hate.
You can choose to be the kind of person that
this moment needs.

And every choice is a signal.
A little flag above your head, declaring:
"This is what I stand for."
"This is who I am."

Some choices are subtle.
How you move through a room.
What you choose not to say.

Some choices are personal.

Like where you spend your money.
Or your memory.
Or your time.

And some choices set new destinies in motion.
Some choices change the world.

But the next choice is always right in front of
you.
Even when you're cornered, you can choose how
to respond.
You can choose how to align yourself against
uncertainty.

To choose courage.
To choose kindness.
To choose dignity.
To choose peace.

And I promise you,
When you meet that moment with humanity,
Those choices will matter.
Those signals will compound.

The world will rearrange itself around the
person that you choose to be.

And everything will bear the signature,
Of the creator you've become.

24.

The shift has already started.
The new world is already being built.

Not by the biggest armies,
Or the deepest pockets,
Or the loudest mouths.

But by the rest of us.
Getting our minds in order.
Putting our hands to work.

The single mom hunched behind a laptop.
The grandfather up at 3 a.m. in his garage.

Little fires.
Scattered in the dark.
We may not see each other,
But together we're illuminating what comes
next.

What can you create today that will serve the
world tomorrow?

Some write.
Some teach.
Some organize.
Some sing.

Some sketch the outlines of a better system.
Some nurture children who will see it through.

Every contribution is important.
Every act of thoughtful craftsmanship creates a
mark.

And over time,
These humble works accumulate and find each
other.
Reinforce each other.
They grow.
They pulse.
They vibrate.
They converge.

They represent the quiet power of committed
people.

Until one day they form a new foundation,
Strong enough to shake the old world to the
ground.

To replace the broken systems.
To unseat the empty leaders that refuse to serve.

And when that day comes, we'll be there to
claim it.

We'll rise.
We'll stand.
We'll flourish.
We'll prevail.

We'll step into a new world,
One that meets our needs with dignity.

Because we took the time to build together.

And create the future we deserve.

25.

And now I ask you to do the hardest thing of all.

The timeless, selfless, thankless thing.

I ask you to keep going.

To hold the vision.
To persist.

I ask you to close this book and take your first
step toward something better.
The first of thousands.
Millions.
A journey that will never end.

Because persistence is the bridge between
believing and becoming something new.
It's the quiet multiplier of conviction.
It can't be cheated.
It can't be rushed.

And although storms will rage,
And doubts will rise,
And weariness will weigh upon your back,

You must keep going.

Like the lighthouse.
Like the heartbeat.
Like the rock.

For you are the axis upon which this world
keeps turning.
Without your faith,
We can't succeed in anything.
But with it,
We cannot fail.

Our transformation is inevitable.

And that fire that you carry will be our beacon.
Our connection to the stars and the centuries
and the source.

Find your way
To take a stand
For being human.

For that's the flame we must keep lit together.

And that's how we're going to save the world.

The End

Thank you for reading *25 Fires*. This book was born in my own personal moment of frustration and despair. I found myself losing faith in a fractured world, and decided to write my way back.

I hope the work meant something to you. I hope it helps you see a little deeper. Sit a little quieter. Stand a little taller.

If you enjoyed this book, I encourage you to pass it on. Find someone in your circle and share a copy or a link. I'm sure it's not for everyone. But it also kind of is.

You can also help by leaving a review, or mentioning the book online. Your simple comment could be the difference in someone else's day. Or mine.

If you're looking for more, let's keep in touch. Head over to **25fires.org** and sign up for my mailing list, or email me directly, **eric@25fires.org** and tell me what you think.

I don't know what the future holds. I can't predict the path from here to there. But I do believe we're on the arc of something greater. And honoring what makes us human will be what scales into a better world.

See you there.

Also by Eric S. Hoffman

Reverend and Raindrop

The Ballad of Clay Moore

*Learn more at **ericshoffman.com***